Look around you
Village

Ruth Thomson

Photography by Chris Fairclough

WAYLAND

First published in 2007 by Wayland

Copyright © Wayland 2007

Wayland
338 Euston Road
London NW1 3BH

Wayland Australia
Hachette Children's Books
Level 17/207 Kent Street
Sydney, NSW 2000

Editor: Victoria Brooker
Designer: Elaine Wilkinson
Design concept: Paul Cherrill

The author and publisher would like to thank: Olly Wales; Picnic Fayre Delicatessen, Cley-next-the-sea; Made in Cley; ©The Image Works/TopFoto for the mobile library picture on page 16.; Jane Hawkins for the cob house pictures on page 11.

British Library Cataloguing in Publication Data

Thomson, Ruth
In a village. – (Look around you)
       1. Villages – Juvenile literature 2. Country life –
       Juvenile literature 3. Human ecology – Juvenile literature
       I.Title
       910.9'1734

ISBN 978 0 7502 5144 0

Printed in China

Wayland is a division of Hachette Children's Books.

Contents

Words in **bold** can be found in the glossary.

Villages everywhere

Villages are small **settlements** surrounded by countryside or by the sea. Most have existed for centuries.

Many villages are in sheltered river **valleys** with rich soil for farming. Others are near coal or tin mines. Some villages cluster around a crossroads or spread out from a shallow river crossing.

▲ Villages are often near a spring or a river, once used for fresh drinking water.

▼ This village sits in a valley, with farmland all around it.

4

Some villages spread out around the foot of a castle or an **abbey**.

Some villages are found where there is a sheltered **bay** or **estuary** for mooring boats.

LOOK CLOSER!

The ending on the name of a place may give a clue about it.

-**ham** and -**ton** both mean village

-**ley** means an open space in a wood

-**ford** means ford (a shallow place to cross a river)

-**wich** means a workplace

Village features

Villages are different shapes. Some are long and thin, with buildings lining both sides of a road.

Some villages have a central green, with a church, pub and old houses around it. Many villages also have a primary school and a shop.

▲ Old houses line the main street of this village.

▼ Local sports, Bonfire Night, village fêtes and other celebrations take place on village greens.

▲ Village shops often have a post office as well. This shop is owned by the villagers, who take it in turns to help run and clean it.

LOOK CLOSER!

What sorts of things does a village shop sell?

Village buildings

Most villages have a church and a pub. Some also have a primary school and a shop. Big villages often have a village hall, as well.

▼ Churches are usually surrounded by a grassy churchyard. Villagers have been buried in their local churchyard for centuries.

▲ Children from several villages attend this primary school. Older pupils travel to a town to go to secondary school.

Pubs may be hundreds of years old. Inns once gave travellers a bed and food for the night.

Village halls are used for local meetings, shows, parties, clubs, playgroups and wedding receptions.

Homes

The oldest houses are usually nearest the centre of a village. Newer ones are on the edges. They nearly all have gardens.

Old houses were built of local, cheap material, such as cob (a mixture of mud and straw), stone, flint, wood or brick.

▲ Some old houses have thatch roofs, made from straw or reed.

◀ New houses, like these, are sometimes built on land that once belonged to a farm.

LOOK CLOSER!

The street names of new housing estates may tell you what the land was once used for.

KINGS ARMS HILL

LOOK CLOSER!

What are old houses in villages in your area built from?

Sandstone

Cob

Stone

Brick

Flint

Work

In the past, people who lived in villages worked there as well and rarely travelled very far.

Nowadays, there are fewer jobs in villages. Many people have to **commute** from their village homes to work in a town or city.

▲ Postmen and women deliver mail by van to villages on their round.

▼ This village farm shop sells all sorts of vegetables grown by local farmers.

◀ This potter makes bowls, plates and jugs in a studio and sells them in her shop next door.

◀ A local groundsman looks after the recreation ground in his village.

LOOK CLOSER!

Find out what jobs people do in a village.
What do people do at the church?
Is there a village doctor, dentist or butcher?

Signs of the past

Until two hundred years ago, most people in Britain lived in villages. Houses had no piped water, so people fetched water from a pump or well.

Most villages had a forge, where a blacksmith made horseshoes and repaired farm machinery. Many villages had a windmill.

▲ Many pumps had a covered shelter, so they could be used in all weathers.

▲ Windmills ground corn into flour or were used as pumps to drain water from the land.

LOOK CLOSER!

Street names often recall places that no longer exist. What historical street names can you find in a village?

WORKHOUSE LANE
LEADING TO
WINDMILL LANE

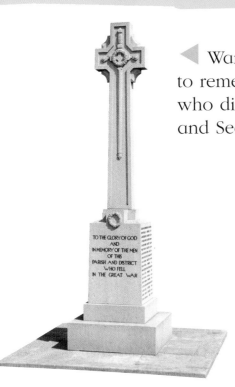

◀ War memorials help us to remember local soldiers who died in the First and Second World Wars.

▶ Market crosses mark the place where a weekly market was once held.

▲ Village ponds were used for watering travellers' horses, as well as the cattle, sheep and pigs being walked to market.

Moving around

Most people who live in villages own cars and travel elsewhere to work, to shop or to places of entertainment. Mobile services, such as doctors or libraries, visit some villages.

Village streets are often narrow and were not designed for cars. Drivers must take care.

▲ Road signs, speed bumps and speed cameras remind cars to slow down through villages.

▶ A mobile library travels from one village to another.

◀ Many villages are on small roads linked to other villages. Villages are often several miles away from the nearest town.

People without cars, such as the young and the elderly, use buses.

Some companies run a bus service which people can call up when they need it.

This bus shelter is also the village noticeboard, where people can put up information about local events.

LOOK CLOSER!

Find out how often a village bus service runs. Is the timetable more useful for workers or for shoppers?

The village church

The village church has always been the heart of village life. In the past, most people walked there for services every Sunday.

People celebrate special days, such as Christmas, Easter and Harvest Festival there.

▶ Some villagers are christened and married in their local church.

LOOK CLOSER!

Look around a village church for features like these. What else can you spot?

Tower with battlements and clock

Wind vane

Gargoyles

Stained glass window

▼ A covered gateway to a churchyard is called a lychgate. Coffins were rested on the wooden platform before burial.

St Mary's · Chiddingfold

SUNDAY 8 a.m. HOLY COMMUNION (BCP)

10 a.m. PARISH COMMUNION with creche and Sunday School, except on the 3rd Sunday in each month, when there will be a FAMILY COMMUNION SERVICE

6.30 p.m. EVENSONG (BCP) 1st Sunday in each month only

WEDNESDAY 9.30 a.m. HOLY COMMUNION

2 p.m. PRAM PRAISE 1st Wednesday in each month only

Rector: Rev Sarah Brough B.Th. The Rectory, Coxcombe Lane, Chiddingfold, GU8 4QA. Telephone 01428 682008 Curate: Rev Gill Welford B.A.(Hons)

Email: stmaryschidd@fish.co.uk

◀ Church signs give the name of the church and the time of services.

LOOK CLOSER!

Look at headstones to find out which families lived in the village for several **generations**.

Mapping a village

Look closely at this map of a village. Notice how:

the crossroads are at the centre of the village

most important buildings, such as the school and village hall, cluster near the crossroads

Some housing is built in no-through roads

▶ School

◀ Church

▶ Shop

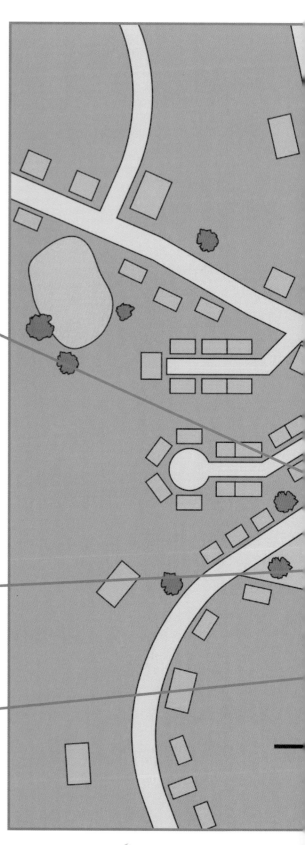

Make a map of a village near where you live.

- Draw the main roads in and out of the village.

- Mark where the church, school, village hall and pub are.

- Mark green spaces, rivers and places of interest.

Crossroads

Village hall

Pub

A walk around a village

Take a walk around a village.
Look for clues that tell you more about it.

▼ ▶ Village signs often highlight an important village building, local activity or historical event.

▼ ▶ Read signs and posters that may tell you about special events or places of interest to visit.

▶ ▲ Village schools are rarer than in the past. If the school has closed down, find out what it has become.

▼ Pubs and cafés are not only places where villagers meet. Discover whether they attract visitors from other villagers and nearby towns.

▲ Notice whether the village has any special facilities for children, such as a playground or a football pitch.

Look at notices at the village hall to see if there are weekly clubs or activities for children.

Glossary

abbey a church built for a community of monks or nuns

bay land on the coast that bends inwards

commute to travel regularly between two places, such as between home and a place of work

estuary the wide mouth of a river

gargoyle a stone-carved ugly creature's head, often found on churches. Its open mouth is a spout for draining rainwater off the roof.

generation a step in a family tree. You are from one generation and your parents are from another.

settlement a place where people have made their homes

valley a stretch of low land between hills, sometimes with a river running through it

Index